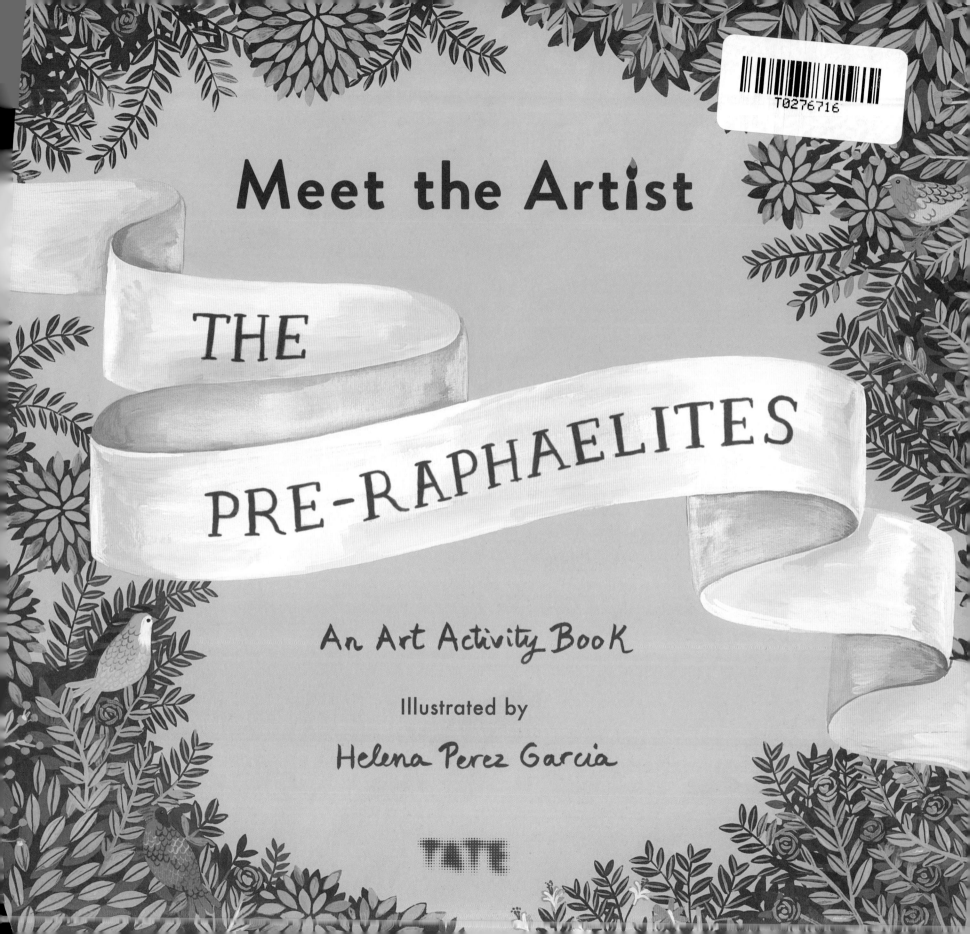

Meet the Artist

THE PRE-RAPHAELITES

An Art Activity Book

Illustrated by

Helena Perez Garcia

TATE

The Pre-Raphaelites were a society of artists founded in London in 1848.
The group was made up of poets, designers, sculptors and painters.

Art at that time was often influenced by Renaissance artists such
as Raphael. The Pre-Raphaelites thought it was boring and wanted
to do something different!

They made art in new ways, using modern life, literature
and the medieval period as their inspiration.

They believed in the idea of 'art for art's sake',
meaning art doesn't need to have a purpose.
It can just be beautiful.

Artist's Advice
'Have nothing in your house
that you do not know to be useful,
or believe to be beautiful.'
William Morris

The Pre-Raphaelites loved to read and write, and many of their paintings were inspired by famous poems and stories.

Ophelia was painted by John Everett Millais and shows a character from the play *Hamlet* by William Shakespeare.

Read the quote from *Hamlet* below.
Can you spot these things in the painting *Ophelia* by Millais?

There is a **willow** grows aslant a **brook**

That shows his hoar **leaves** in the glassy **stream**.

There with fantastic garlands did she come

Of **crow-flowers**, **nettles**, **daisies**, and long purples

William Shakespeare

In the Victorian period, people believed that flowers had special meanings.
Artists would include flowers in their paintings to show different moods and emotions.

Use colouring pencils to draw flowers
that you feel match these words.

Dante Gabriel Rossetti was one of the founding members of the Pre-Raphaelites. He used his friends and family as models, dressed up as different characters. In his painting *Proserpine* his friend Jane Morris is dressed as an Ancient Roman goddess who was kidnapped and taken to the underworld.

Objects in the painting give us clues about her story.

The pomegranate represents being trapped.

The incense burner shows she is a goddess.

The ivy is a symbol of memory. She misses her home!

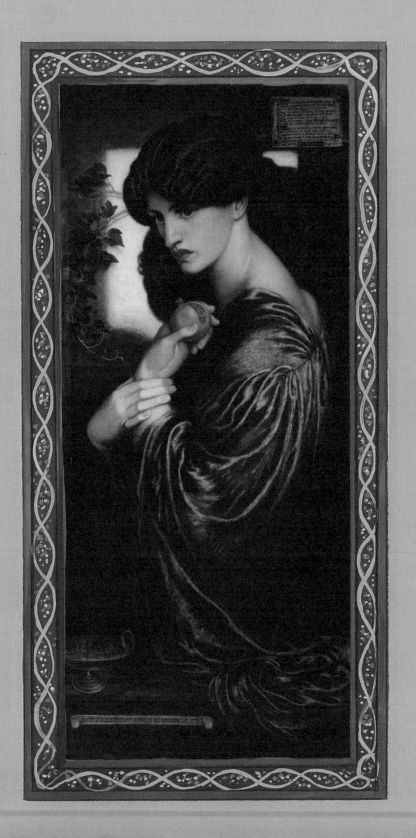

Draw a portrait of someone you know here. It could be a family member, a friend or even a character from a book or movie! Include objects that show their personality. Do they like sports? Do they have a favourite animal? Think about what you want the drawing to say about the person.

Remember to add as much detail as possible!

The Pre-Raphaelites studied their models very carefully to make sure they got their faces just right. Proportion is very important when it comes to drawing faces.

Draw a cross, then sketch an oval shape around the cross. This will be your face!

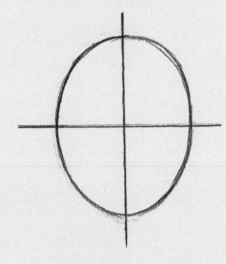

Draw two almond shapes for eyes on either side of the vertical line.

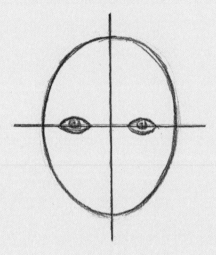

Between the chin and the eyes, draw another horizontal line. On this line draw your nose.

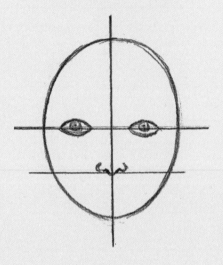

Just below the nose, draw a third horizontal line and add your mouth.

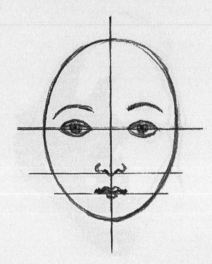

Add some eyebrows above the eyes.

Now for the hair! What style will you choose?

Now draw your own face here. Don't forget to use a mirror or take a selfie!

Julia Margaret Cameron was a photographer who used her family to stage scenes from medieval tales. In *So like a shatter'd Column lay the King* she illustrated a poem by Alfred Tennyson about the legend of King Arthur.

Draw a picture of your family or friends eating lunch.

Now draw the same
people as . . .

Tudors

Victorians

Romans

Think about the clothing
people would have worn.
You can use books and
the internet to help you.

The Pre-Raphaelites were very interested in the idea of being true to nature.
They tried to paint landscapes as accurately as possible.

They collected flora and fauna that they found in the countryside
then took them back to their studios to study.

Can you collect the following objects and stick them here?

Blade of grass

Leaf

Tree bark

Feather

Now make drawings
of each object
in these boxes.

Blade of grass

Leaf

Tree bark

Feather

This painting by William Holman Hunt is called
Our English Coasts, 1852 ('Strayed Sheep').
Some people have said it looks like a photograph
because it's so detailed, but this image isn't what it seems!
Hunt painted each plant and animal from
real-life examples, then brought them together
to create this painting, almost like a collage.

Top Tip!

Make sure to take your photos
from lots of different angles!

Go into your garden or a park and take lots of photographs.
You could take a photo of a tree, a bench,
the lawn or even the sky. Now print these photos out,
cut them up, then stick them back together
to make a whole new landscape!

As well as the countryside,
the Pre-Raphaelites were inspired by
the modern cities in which they lived.

In this painting called Work the artist,
Ford Madox Brown, has included a lot of
different jobs. How many can you spot?

SWEETS
&
SNACKS

Draw yourself doing your dream job. What do you want to be?
Where would you work? In an office, a zoo or even a spaceship?

The Pre-Raphaelites included some very important women. Joanna Mary Wells, Elizabeth Siddal, Julia Margaret Cameron and Christina Rossetti each used different mediums to tell their stories.

The painting opposite, Sir Patrick Spens by Elizabeth Siddal, is based on an ancient Scottish poem and shows a group of women staring out to sea.

Write a story to describe what is happening in the painting.

Who is your favourite character from a book? Draw them here.

Who do you think these women are, and why they are waiting on the beach?

Amor Mundi

Christina Rossetti was a poet and writer. Her most famous work is a long poem called *Goblin Market* about two sisters and their adventures at an enchanted fruit market. Her brother, Dante Gabriel, illustrated the poem.

Christina Rossetti also wrote the poem below. Read it then illustrate it here. You can use paints, colouring pencils or crayons. Be sure to use lots of colour!

Colour

What is pink? a rose is pink

By the fountain's brink.

What is red? a poppy's red

In its barley bed.

What is blue? the sky is blue

Where the clouds float thro'.

What is white? a swan is white

Sailing in the light.

What is yellow? pears are yellow,

Rich and ripe and mellow.

What is green? the grass is green,

With small flowers between.

What is violet? clouds are violet

In the summer twilight.

What is orange? why, an orange,

Just an orange!

Christina Rossetti

This painting by Edward Burne-Jones is called *Sidonia von Bork 1560*. Sidonia was supposedly a witch who was so beautiful she could enchant people with her looks.

When Burne-Jones painted clothing, he included lots of different fabrics, patterns and jewels to show each character's personality. In this painting Sidonia's dress is patterned with snaking lines like a giant net!

Design your own outfits here. You could draw an outfit for a friend.
Think about what you want the clothes to say about them and their personality.

The Pre-Raphaelites weren't just painters.
William Morris was a designer who made furniture,
and designed patterns for wallpaper and fabrics.
His patterns could be repeated again and again,
using a technique called wood-block printing.

Make your own wallpaper!

You will need:

- Paper - potato - paint
- paper towel - sponge cloth
- an adult to help you!

1. Ask an adult to cut a potato in half.
2. Next, get the adult to help you cut out a simple shape, like a diamond or a leaf. The shape should be raised, like a stamp.
3. Leave your potato to dry on a paper towel with the cut side down.
4. Once dry, apply paint to the shape cut into the potato.
5. Now simply press your potato stamp down onto the paper that you want to decorate to make a pattern.

Top tip!
Make potato stamps in lots of different shapes!

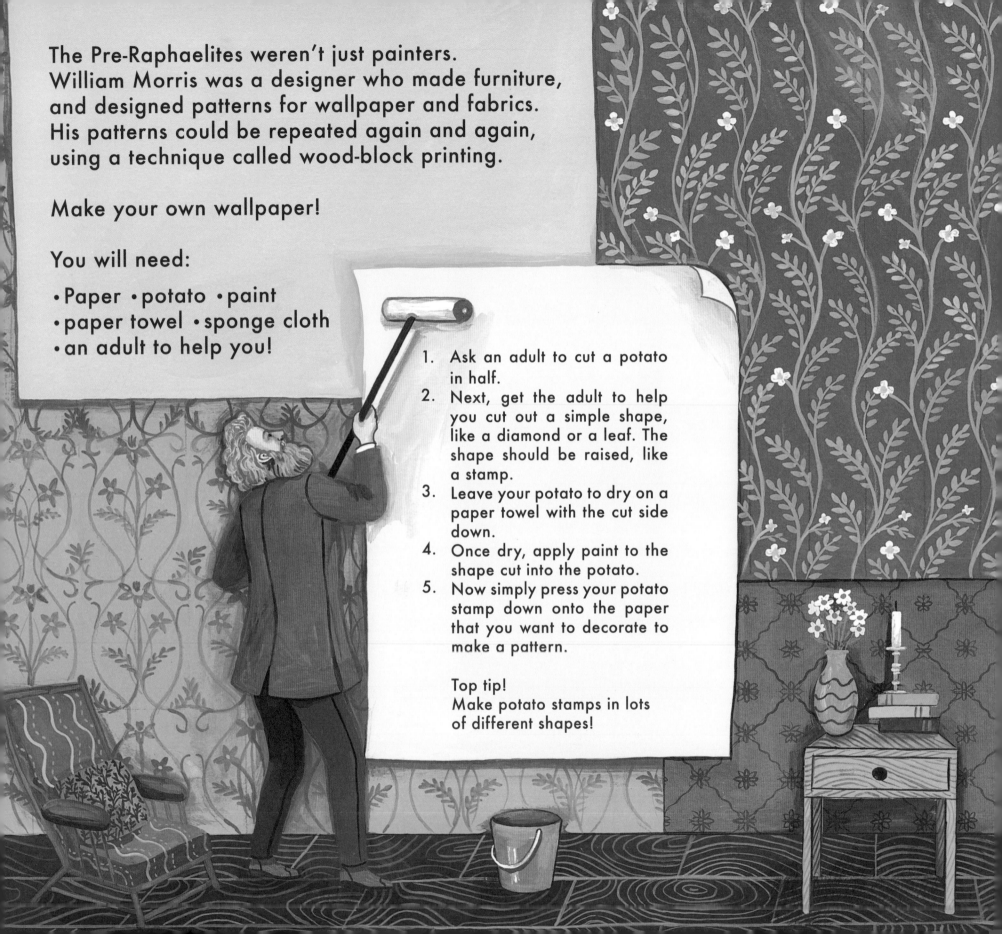

Practise your potato stamps here!

You can make your own stained-glass window too! First, take a piece of black card and carefully cut out patterns and shapes. Next, stick pieces of coloured tissue paper to the back of the card. Finally, hold it up to the light and admire your creation!

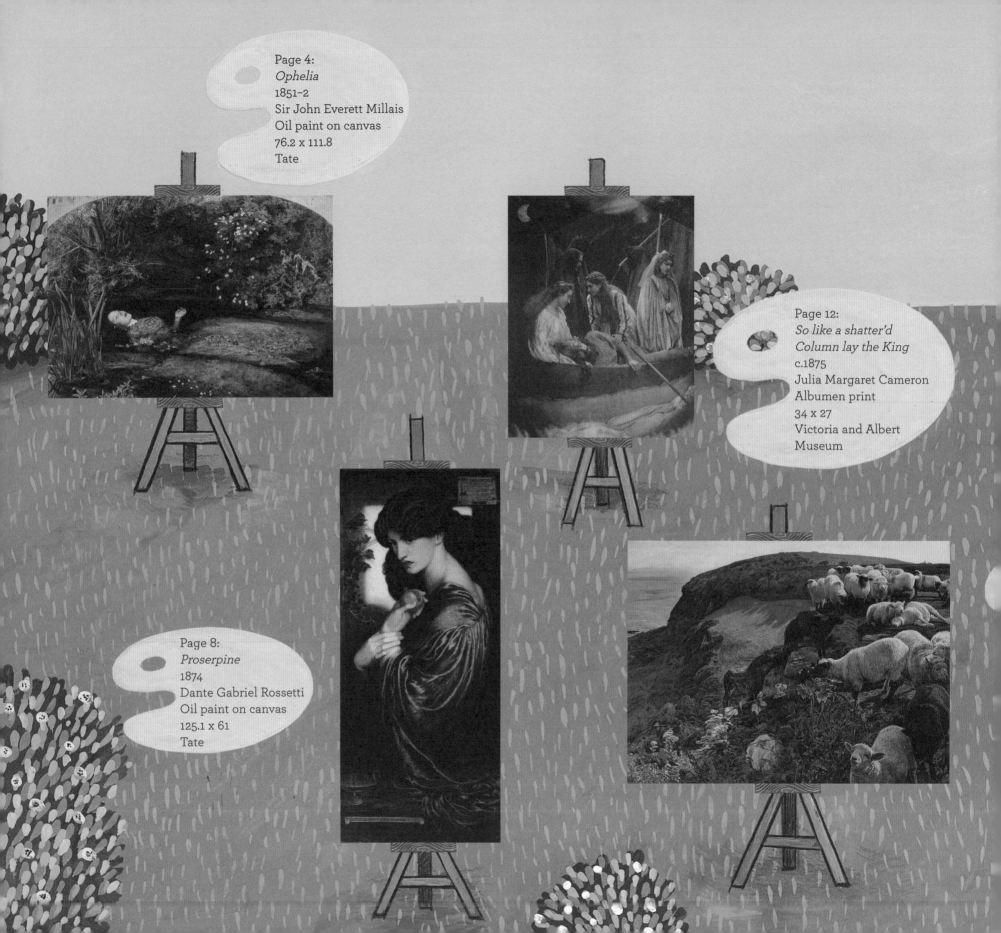

Page 4:
Ophelia
1851–2
Sir John Everett Millais
Oil paint on canvas
76.2 x 111.8
Tate

Page 12:
So like a shatter'd
Column lay the King
c.1875
Julia Margaret Cameron
Albumen print
34 x 27
Victoria and Albert
Museum

Page 8:
Proserpine
1874
Dante Gabriel Rossetti
Oil paint on canvas
125.1 x 61
Tate

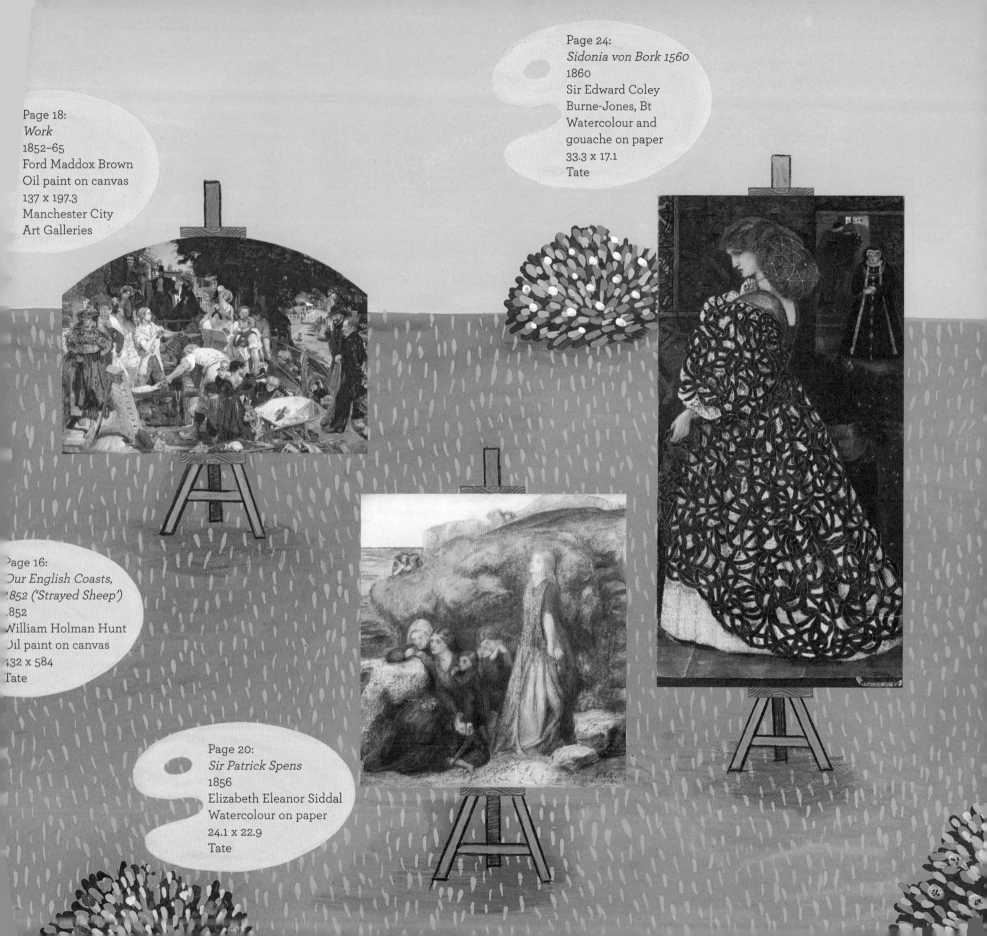

Page 18:
Work
1852–65
Ford Maddox Brown
Oil paint on canvas
137 x 197.3
Manchester City
Art Galleries

Page 24:
Sidonia von Bork 1560
1860
Sir Edward Coley
Burne-Jones, Bt
Watercolour and
gouache on paper
33.3 x 17.1
Tate

Page 16:
*Our English Coasts,
1852 ('Strayed Sheep')*
1852
William Holman Hunt
Oil paint on canvas
432 x 584
Tate

Page 20:
Sir Patrick Spens
1856
Elizabeth Eleanor Siddal
Watercolour on paper
24.1 x 22.9
Tate

With special thanks to Pablo

First published 2018 by order of the Tate Trustees
by Tate Publishing, a division of Tate Enterprises Ltd,
Millbank, London SW1P 4RG
www.tate.org.uk/publishing

Photo credits:
Page 12: © Victoria and Albert Museum, London
Page 18: Manchester Art Gallery, UK / Bridgeman Images
Pages 4, 8, 16, 20, 24 © Tate

A catalogue record for this book is available from the British Library

ISBN 978 1 84976 591 6

Distributed in the United States and Canada by ABRAMS, New York
Library of Congress Control Number applied for

Colour reproduction by DL Imaging, London
Printed in China by Toppan Leefung Printing Ltd.

Measurements of artworks are given in centimetres, height before width